Activities We Do

We Learn at School

by Connor Stratton

FOCUS READERS

SCOUT

www.focusreaders.com

Focus Readers is distributed by North Star Editions:
sales@northstareditions.com | 888-417-0195

Produced for Focus Readers by Red Line Editorial.

Photographs ©: michaeljung/Shutterstock Images, cover, 1; FatCamera/iStockphoto, 4 (top); PeopleImages/iStockphoto, 4 (bottom); LightField Studios/Shutterstock Images, 7, 16 (bottom right); GagliardiPhotography/Shutterstock Images, 9 (top); Rawpixel.com/Shutterstock Images, 9 (bottom); Monkey Business Images/Shutterstock Images, 11 (top), 16 (top left); Ridofranz/iStockphoto, 11 (bottom); SpeedKingz/Shutterstock Images, 13; Bangkok Click Studio/Shutterstock Images, 15, 16 (bottom left); zhengzaishuru/iStockphoto, 16 (top right)

Library of Congress Cataloging-in-Publication Data
Library of Congress Cataloging-in-Publication Data is available on the Library of Congress website.

ISBN
978-1-64185-799-4 (hardcover)
978-1-64185-868-7 (paperback)
978-1-64185-994-3 (ebook pdf)
978-1-64185-937-0 (hosted ebook)

Printed in the United States of America
Mankato, MN
May, 2019

About the Author

Connor Stratton enjoys learning new things, eating popcorn, and watching movies with friends. He lives in Minnesota.

Table of Contents

teacher

School Is Fun

We learn at school.

We learn to read.

We read with our teacher.

We read by ourselves.

We learn to write.

We write with a **pencil**.

We write on paper.

pencil

Learning Math

We learn math at school.

We learn about numbers.

We learn about shapes.

3 x 9 =
4 x 3 =
number

shape

We learn to add.

We add **blocks**.

We add numbers.

block

Science Every Day

We learn science at school.

We use a **microscope**.

Small things look big.

microscope

We mix things in a bowl.
The bowl fills with **foam**.
We learn what happened.
We learn at school
every day.

foam
bowl

Glossary

blocks

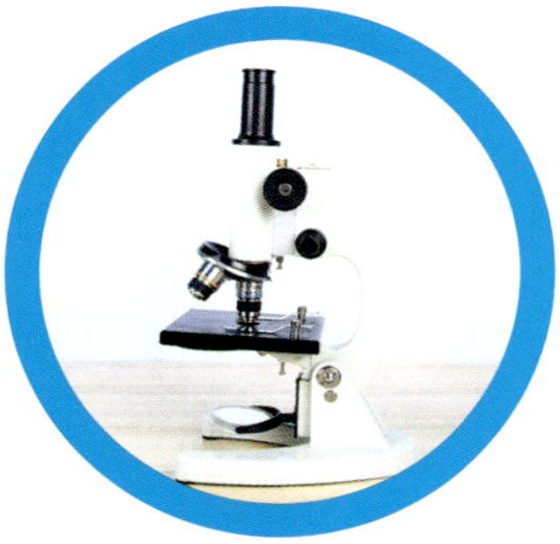

microscope

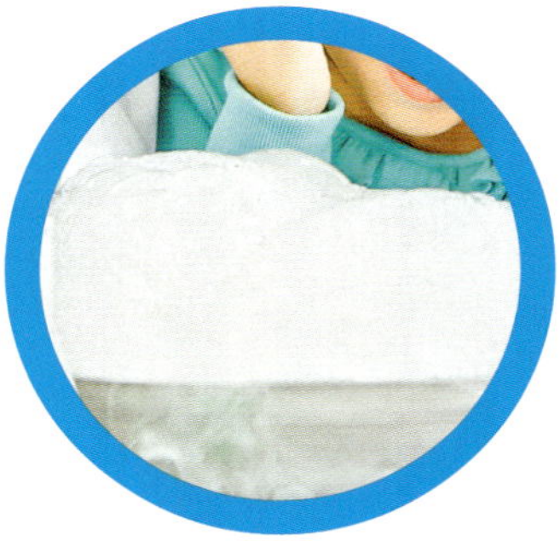

foam

pencil

Index